Our Changing World

THE HISTORY OF THE AIRPLANE

BY BARBARA A. SOMERVILL

| 1850 | 1900 | 1950 | 2000 | 2050 |

Content Adviser: Dorothy Cochrane, Curator, Aeronautics Division, Smithsonian Institution, Washington, D.C.

THE CHILD'S WORLD® • CHANHASSEN, MINNESOTA

HOW DOES IT FLY?

"We're going where?" Marisol asked.

"Papi has a new job in Ithaca, New York," explained Mami. "We're going to fly there."

Oooh, this did not sound good. In her short life, Marisol had never been outside Texas. She didn't want to go now. And she definitely didn't want to go on an airplane.

Travel day arrived much too soon. At the gate, Marisol watched workers load suitcases, food, and cargo on the plane. An attendant called for rows 11 through 20. Marisol's family boarded and found their seats.

People filled the plane and buckled their seat belts. The plane backed away from the gate. As the jet engines roared to life, the plane shook. Marisol squeezed her eyes shut. The plane rushed forward, faster and faster.

Wing and body design help lift this heavy jet into the air.

"Open your eyes, Marisol," said Mami. "We're flying." It seemed impossible. The airplane, passengers, and cargo weighed tons. Marisol wondered, "How could it fly?"

CHAPTER ONE

DREAMS OF FLIGHT

Ancient Greeks told the tale of Daedalus and his son Icarus. In about 1700 B.C., King Minos had Daedalus build a huge maze. It became the king's jail for the Minotaur, half man and half bull. One day, Minos became angry with Daedalus and put the engineer and his son in the maze, too.

To escape, Daedalus built wings of wax and feathers. He warned Icarus not to fly too high. Father and son escaped the maze by flying out over the sea. But Icarus did not listen to his father. He soared upward until the sun melted his wax wings. The boy fell to earth and died.

There is a moral to this story from mythology: Earth is for man; the sky belongs to the gods. Yet, humans have long gazed in wonder at birds and bees and dragonflies. And they have asked why humans could not fly, too.

6

1700 B.C.

The Greek myth of Daedalus and Icarus tells of men flying.

Abraham, known as the father of the Jewish people, is living at this time.

Along South America's west coast, the Nazca culture rose between 400 B.C. and A.D. 900. The Nazca wove cloth so tight it held air. Nazca pottery and pictures in tombs show men "flying" in something that looks like hot air balloons. The Nazca had a legend of a flying boy and stories that claim men flew over enemy armies.

400 B.C.– A.D.1300: FLYING FAILURES

Balloons, gliders, and kites became the first means of flight for humans. In 400 B.C., Archytas of Greece experimented with small gliders. He created a "flying dove," a wooden glider that had a birdlike shape. The glider was a small model, but it could fly.

In A.D. 559, Chinese emperor Kao Yang experimented

The Greek mathematician Archytas experimented with toy gliders.

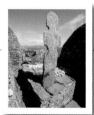

A.D. 559

Emperor Kao Yang experiments with manned kites.

Ireland, know as the island of saints and scholars, sends missionaries to educate the people in England, Scotland, and France.

with flying manned kites. He used prisoners as "test pilots" for these kites. The flights were reasonably successful, although many pilots died. The Chinese used the manned kites to spy on their enemies.

In 1300, Italian explorer Marco Polo wrote about seeing manned kites in China. By then, merchants were using the kites as fortune-tellers. Business travelers did not want to sail on a losing venture or a doomed ship. The crews seized men and lashed them to the kites. If a kite flew straight, that meant the business trip would be successful. Merchants would then quickly sign on with the ship.

1492: LEONARDO'S DREAMS

Leonardo da Vinci was a gifted painter, scientist, and inventor.

| 1010 | Eilmer crashes while flapping wings attached to his body.

Norsemen sail to North America and build the settlement of Vinland. | 1300 | Marco Polo writes about manned kites in China.

Eyeglasses become common in Europe. |

Da Vinci was truly one of the great minds of the 15th and 16th centuries. In 1492, he designed his first flying machine. During his life, he produced 500 sketches of flying machines and wrote more than 35,000 words on his ideas about flight.

Da Vinci built and tested a model helicopter that he called an ornithopter. His design was close to the actual design of the first successful helicopter—developed about 400 years later.

Da Vinci also invented an item no pilot should fly without—the parachute. His parachute design would later allow humans to reach the ground safely from great heights.

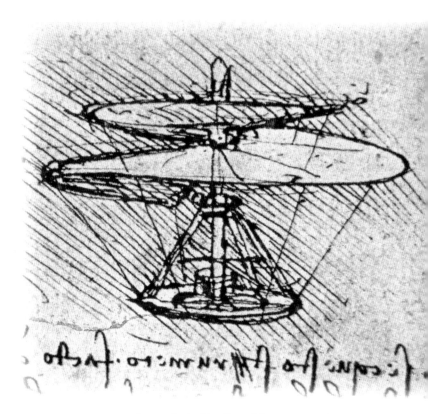

Leonardo da Vinci's ornithopter inspired today's helicopter.

1492	Leonardo da Vinci designs the first of 500 flying machine ideas.
	Christopher Columbus (left) sails westward and proves the earth is not flat.

CHAPTER TWO

FLY, FLY AGAIN

Betwen da Vinci's great ideas and the era of successful flying came many disasters. Hopeful fliers believed, "If at first you don't succeed, fly, fly again."

Overly enthusiastic men—no women—thought wings would make them flight-worthy. They leaped off towers, castles, and church steeples. In 1507, John Damian jumped off Stirling Castle in Scotland. He blamed his failure to fly—and several broken bones—on his use of chicken feathers. Chickens, after all, cannot fly.

Pilots built wings of varying shapes and sizes. In Paris, the Marquis de Bacqueville attached rounded wings to his arms and legs. Looking like an overgrown dragonfly, he set to the air above the Seine River. He crashed on a laundry barge mid-river.

1507

Damian leaps off Stirling Castle and crashes.

Martin Waldseemuller, a mapmaker, calls the "New World" America.

1783: BALLOONING

The first European success for hot air balloons came with the Montgolfier brothers in 1783. Joseph and Etienne Montgolfier built and flew several test balloons before allowing a human rider. On their second trial, the brothers sent up a rooster, duck, and sheep.

The first two men to fly in a Montgolfier balloon were Jean-Francois Pilatre de Rozier and Francois Laurent, the Marquis d'Arlandes. Their flight on November 21, 1783, lasted about four minutes.

Balloon rides became popular events. Fairs offered rides in balloons that were tied securely to the ground. During the Civil War, the Union army

Up, up, and away went the Mongolfier brothers' hot air balloon.

 1783

Joseph Montgolfier (right) and Etienne Montgolfier send a sheep, a rooster, and a duck on a balloon flight.

The *Pennsylvania Evening Post* becomes the first daily newspaper published in the United States.

11

used hot air balloons to spy on Confederate troops. Pilots got a bird's-eye view of enemy locations, troop size, and weapons.

1799–1850s: GLIDERS

British scientist Sir George Cayley studied wing shape and air moving over wings. For his work, he is considered the father of **aerodynamics.** For 50 years, Cayley designed and built gliders. After years of experiments, Cayley decided that without an engine, a glider could not hope to propel a person into the air over any distance.

That doesn't mean that glider fans did not try. In the late 1800s, German engineer Otto Lilienthal designed a glider big enough to carry a person. His glider

1799

Sir George Cayley begins studying wing design.

George Washington (right) dies at his home, Mount Vernon.

also traveled short distances. Lilienthal's ideas about flight helped Wilbur and Orville Wright build their plane.

1852: BLIMPS

In 1852, Henri Giffard, a French inventor, attached a steam engine to a balloon and invented the blimp. His blimp was 145 feet (44 m) long and was the first balloon-like vessel to have steering.

Blimps attracted the attention of Brazilian Alberto Santos-Dumont, who first flew in a balloon in 1898. Santos-Dumont immediately began building **dirigibles** like Giffard's. In 1901,

Otto Lilienthal, a pioneer of modern flight, gets ready for take-off.

1852	Henri Giffard designs a blimp with steering ability.

Elisha Otis (right) invents the elevator.

Santos-Dumont circled the Eiffel Tower in Paris on his airship. He won a cash prize for being the first to fly around the tower. Brazilians honor Santos-Dumont—and not the Wright Brothers—as the first person to "fly" an airship.

With a large enough **gondola,** blimps could carry passengers. During the early 1900s, Count von Zeppelin experimented with shapes and sizes of dirigibles. He tried various gases, such as helium and hydrogen, to raise the blimps. Zeppelins, as they were called, became a common means of transportation. They fell from favor when the *Hindenburg* caught fire in 1937, killing 36 people.

While blimps were growing in popularity, two brothers were working on a flying machine in their

1898

Alberto Santos-Dumont (right) takes his first flight in a balloon.

Spain declares war on the United States.

Dayton, Ohio, bicycle shop. They studied glider shapes and the efforts of balloonists. They read Lilienthal's papers and studied *Progress in Flying Machines* by Octave Chanute. The brothers were Wilbur and Orville Wright. Within three years of Santos-Dumont's fabulous flight, the Wrights would go down in history.

1937

The *Hindenburg* catches fire, and 36 people die.

George VI becomes king of Great Britain.

Zeppelins became less popular after the Hindenburg *caught fire and crashed in 1937.*

CHAPTER THREE

WILBUR AND ORVILLE TAKE OFF

While Wilbur and Orville Wright fixed bent bicycle spokes, their minds soared through the air. They began their pursuit of flight just like early humans—by watching birds. However, the Wrights noticed something that others missed. Birds bent and curved their wings for different flying patterns. The Wrights decided that they, too, could fly if they could make curved wings.

In 1899, the Wrights wrote to the Smithsonian Institution in Washington, D.C. They wanted to learn everything they could about flying. They studied the work of Cayley, Chanute, Lilienthal, and Samuel Langley. They added their own ideas about wings to the findings of earlier "fliers."

For the next few years, the Wrights built gliders. They decided that making

1899

Wilbur and Orville Wright (right) begin studying and designing gliders.

Aspirin is the "wonder drug" sold in pharmacies.

the correct wing shape was important. The brothers tested their designs, such as kites, on strong ropes.

1900: GLIDER TESTING

In 1900, Wilbur and Orville built and tested one of their largest gliders. The wings stretched 17 feet (5 m), and the glider weighed 52 pounds (24 kilograms). The brothers added a wing-shaping device that allowed the wings to curve as the glider flew.

The Wrights chose North Carolina's Outer Banks as a test site. The area had high sand dunes and plenty of wind to help with launching. The Wrights tested the glider with and without a pilot. Their success led them to plan a bigger, better glider.

Wilbur Wright practiced flying in a glider before he and Orville built the first airplane.

1900

The Wrights test a wing-shaping device.

Hawaii officially becomes a territory of the United States.

"To invent an airplane . . . is nothing. To build an airplane . . . is something. But to fly . . . is everything."
Otto Lilienthal, German glider designer

The Wrights used a wind tunnel to help improve wing design on their gliders.

The following year, the Wrights tested a new glider at Kill Devil Hills on the Outer Banks near the town of Kitty Hawk. This glider's wings stretched 22 feet (6.7 m). The brothers added another **innovation**—landing gear. This time, their glider pitched and fell. It did not have enough power to truly get off the ground.

The Wrights realized a bigger glider needed an engine. They also saw that their designs had flaws. The curved wings did not work as well as bird wings. The gliders shifted and spun out of control. Wilbur and Orville decided to build a wind tunnel. They tested different wing shapes in the tunnel. The best design became part of a new 32-foot (10-m) wing glider.

1900

The Wrights build a wind tunnel to improve wing designs.

President William McKinley is shot and dies after only a few months in office.

1903: FIRST IN FLIGHT

In the fall of 1903, the Wrights designed an airplane called the *Flyer*. This airplane weighed between 600 and 700 pounds (272 and 318 kg). It had a powerful engine to thrust the plane into the air.

To help the plane take off, the Wrights built a wood ramp. The ramp helped the plane pick up enough speed for takeoff. The Wrights believed their heavier plane could fly.

Orville Wright's first flight lasted 12 seconds. The Wright *Flyer* traveled just 121 feet (37 m). The plane was so slow that Wilbur easily ran alongside it. Still, this was the first successful powered, piloted, heavier-than-air flight.

THE WRIGHT BROTHERS FLIPPED A COIN TO SEE WHO WOULD BE THE FIRST TEST PILOT. WILBUR WON, BUT HIS DECEMBER 14 FLIGHT FAILED. ORVILLE'S TURN CAME ON DECEMBER 17, 1903. BEING SECOND GOT ORVILLE'S NAME IN THE RECORD BOOKS. WILBUR FLEW AFTER ORVILLE THAT SAME DAY. THEY EACH MADE ONE MORE FLIGHT THAT DAY.

1903

Orville Wright makes the first successful manned, powered, heavier-than-air flight.

Teddy bears, named for President Teddy Roosevelt (right), go on sale.

A year later, Wilbur took his turn at the controls of the 1904 *Flyer* and managed a five-minute flight. In 1905, the Wrights had pushed their flight time up to 40 minutes.

1909: THE WRIGHT COMPANY

For the next several years, the Wrights built and flew airplanes. They began carrying passengers, which attracted more attention to their flying. In 1905, the brothers contacted the United States government about buying an airplane. Their request was rejected.

However, government opinion changed. In 1909, the Wrights sold a **biplane** to the government for $25,000. The United States now had an air force of one plane.

1909

The U.S. government begins its air force with one plane.

The National Association for the Advancement of Colored People (NAACP) is formed.

1911

The *Vin Fiz* crosses the United States in 84 days.

Willis Carrier (left) invents the air conditioner.

CHAPTER FOUR

BIGGER, FASTER, SAFER AIRPLANES

By 1910, flight became a familiar event. More people got pilot's licenses or took rides as passengers in the 1920s. Most landings were little more than controlled crashes. Lucky pilots walked away. Unlucky ones wound up in hospitals or funeral parlors.

Real advances in airplane design came with World War I (1914–1918). In 1914, both sides had few airplanes. Those planes were used to spy on the enemy. It then occurred to someone that pilots could drop bombs. To bomb targets, pilots leaned over and looked down. They grabbed a bomb and dropped it.

The war progressed slowly. Both armies were bogged down in trenches, and thousands of men died. Then a new form of warfare became popular—dogfights in the air. The term *dogfight* describes close combat between two planes.

Harriet Quimby (right) becomes the first American woman with a pilot's license.

Roald Amundsen reaches the South Pole.

1911

War planes needed quick, dramatic changes to be effective. By 1914, it was possible for pilots to be able to talk to their ground support over radios, though this was not yet widespread. Later, pilots were able to talk from plane to plane by radio. Airplane bodies went from wood to stronger metal. Engines became more powerful, making planes faster. Pilots performed banked turns and loop-the-loops. These flying techniques became popular at air shows and county fairs. But they began as ways to avoid enemy bullets.

During the war, airplane use changed from spy planes to war planes. Dogfights became a new form of battle. By the time World War I ended, about 150,000 planes had been downed in military action.

1914

World War I opens with a total air force of about 1,000 planes.

The Panama Canal is completed.

1918–1939: FLYING BECOMES BUSINESS

The U.S. Post Office recognized how airplanes could speed up the mail. In 1918, the Post Office tried its first airmail deliveries. Two years later, they were flying mail from New York to San Francisco. The journey took 33 hours and 20 minutes—three days faster than delivery by train. Soon, the Post Office issued its first airmail stamps. They cost just 10 cents.

Airlines opened for business and took passengers on rather shaky trips from city to city. By the 1930s, planes with **automatic pilots** made flying and landing safer. By 1938, **pressurized** cabins made flying at high altitudes possible.

1918	U.S. airmail begins delivery.
	Daylight saving time goes into effect for the first time.

In 1929, airplane travel made flying to exotic places such as Cuba easy.

So many people were flying that the skies became crowded and dangerous. Air traffic control became the way to keep planes from crashing into each other. Controllers told pilots when to take off, at what height to fly, and when they could land.

The 1936 invention of jet engines changed air travel forever. During the 1940s and 1950s, engineers experimented with jet engines on airplanes. By the 1960s, coast-to-coast passenger flights took only five or six hours.

1923–TODAY: MAKING AND BREAKING RECORDS

Pilots always wanted to go faster, higher, longer, farther. They hoped to make new records and break old ones.

1923

The first nonstop, coast-to-coast airplane trip takes place between New York and San Diego.

President Warren Harding dies while in office; Calvin Coolidge (right) becomes the new president.

In the 1920s and 1930s, these records made front-page news.

In 1923, the first nonstop, coast-to-coast airplane trip went from New York to San Diego. The trip lasted 26 hours and 50 minutes. And that was a speed record! Of course, round-the-world records followed. The first round-the-world trip was completed in Seattle, Washington, in 1924. In 1927, Charles Lindbergh's picture appeared in every newspaper. He flew his *Spirit of Saint Louis* single-handedly across the Atlantic.

1927	Charles Lindbergh arrives in Paris after flying solo across the Atlantic Ocean.
	Wings receives the first Academy Award (Oscar) for best picture.

Charles Lindbergh flew the Spirit of Saint Louis *from New York to Paris, France.*

During World War II, U.S. planes bombed Hokadate, Japan.

The beginning of World War II in 1939 brought other changes in airplane design. Gigantic bombers carried deadly payloads that flattened enemy towns. Soldiers crossed the oceans in planes, arriving at battle scenes within days. Planes took off and landed on massive aircraft carriers. These huge ships became "instant airports" on open oceans.

In 1947, flying reached a new level. On October 14, Chuck Yeager flew an X-1 jet faster than the speed of sound and broke the sound barrier for the first time. Yeager reached speeds of 700 miles per hour (1,127 kph). What a change from the Wrights' *Flyer* that flew so slowly Wilbur Wright could run along beside it.

1947

Chuck Yeager breaks the sound barrier.

Jackie Robinson becomes the first African-American major league baseball player.

CHAPTER FIVE

AIRPLANES TODAY AND TOMORROW

At Boeing, a major airplane builder, engineers use computers to model and test new planes. Computers compare different metals and plastics. The company also thinks about human safety and comfort in plane design. This is a big change from 100 years ago.

Planes for the military have changed, too. Today, the U.S. Air Force has stealth bombers that zip through the skies undetected by radar. Computers "pilot" unmanned planes into combat zones. New planes, called X-35Bs, take off straight up like helicopters and can hover like hummingbirds.

2000s: WHAT IS NEXT?

One hundred years ago, the Wright brothers' first flight thrilled the world. One hundred years from now, families will probably travel by "air-car." Highways to

2000

1.58 billion passengers travel on the world's airlines.

Children everywhere read *Harry Potter and the Sorcerer's Stone*.

This plane of the future features "Smart Wings" that self-adjust during flight.

and from school or work will be 50 feet (15 m) above the ground.

Today, the National Aeronautics and Space Administration (NASA) is developing airplane wings that bend and curve like bird wings. Using computers and space-age materials, they are developing "smart wings." These wings will adjust to changes in flight patterns the way birds do.

The material used to build future planes will heal itself. A bullet ripping through a wing will no longer

2002

The *Spirit of Freedom* balloon circles the globe.

Friends is the most-watched show on television.

matter. Within seconds, the material will self-repair, and the wing will be perfect again.

NASA studies biomimetics—ways of copying what occurs in nature. For example, bird bones are both strong and lightweight. They have hard surfaces but have air pockets inside. Scientists want to put tiny spheres inside metal when it is made. When the metal hardens, the inside layer will be like bird bones. Hopefully, it will also be strong.

Planes fly higher and go faster. They can travel longer. Yet, for all the advances airplanes have enjoyed, they still cannot soar like eagles, swoop like falcons, or flit like hummingbirds. Humans have solved the mystery of flight. But they have not taken away its wonder.

2003

The X-35B (right) becomes the latest military weapon.

The United States and its allies invade Iraq.

aerodynamics (air-oh-dye-NAM-miks)
Aerodynamics is the study of air moving over surfaces, such as plane wings or cars. Sir George Cayley is considered the father of aerodynamics.

automatic pilots (aw-tuh-MAT-ik PYE-luhts)
Automatic pilots are instruments that can fly planes without human aid. Planes with automatic pilots made flying and landing safer.

biplane (BYE-plane) A biplane is a plane with upper and lower wings. In 1909, the Wrights' biplane became the first plane in the government's air force.

dirigibles (DIHR-uh-juh-buhlz) Dirigibles are a type of blimp. Count von Zeppelin experimented with shapes and sizes of dirigibles.

gondola (GON-duh-luh) A gondola on a blimp is the basket or pilot's area. A duck, a sheep, and a rooster rode in the gondola of the Montgolfier brothers' balloon.

innovation (in-uh-VAY-shuhn) An innovation is a new idea. Adding landing gear to an airplane was a clever innovation in the 1900s.

pressurized (PRESH-uh-rized) Pressurized means to maintain a normal, ground-level atmosphere in an area, such as an airplane cabin. Thanks to a pressurized cabin, a plane can fly at high altitudes with no problems.

FOR FURTHER INFORMATION

AT THE LIBRARY
Nonfiction
Burkett, Molly. *Pioneers of the Air.* Hauppauge, N.Y.: Barron's Educational Series, 1998.

Gunston, Bill. *The World of Flight.* Milwaukee: Gareth Stevens, 2001.

Jennings, Terry. *Planes, Gliders, Helicopters: And Other Flying Machines.* New York: Kingfisher, 1993.

Jerome, Kate Boehm. *Who Was Amelia Earhart?* New York: Grosset & Dunlap, 2002.

* Nathan, Amy. *Yankee Doodle Gals: Women Pilots of World War II.* Washington, D.C.: National Geographic, 2001.

* Stevenson, Augusta. *Wilbur and Orville Wright: Young Fliers.* New York: Aladdin Library, 1986.

Fiction
Gutman, Dan. *Race for the Sky: The Kitty Hawk Diaries of Johnny Moore.* New York: Simon & Schuster, 2003.

Books marked with a star are challenge reading material for those reading above grade level.

ON THE WEB
Visit our home page for lots of links about airplanes: *http://www.childsworld.com/links.html*

Note to Parents, Teachers, and Librarians:
We routinely check our Web links to make sure they're safe, active sites—so encourage your readers to check them out!

PLACES TO VISIT OR CONTACT
National Air and Space Museum
6th and Independence Avenue SW
Washington, DC 20560

Wright Brothers National Memorial
1401 National Park Drive
Manteo, NC 27954

99s Museum of Women Pilots
4300 Amelia Earhart Road
Oklahoma City, OK 73159

INDEX

ABOUT THE AUTHOR

BARBARA A. SOMERVILL IS THE AUTHOR OF MANY BOOKS FOR CHILDREN. SHE LOVES LEARNING AND SEES EVERY WRITING PROJECT AS A CHANCE TO LEARN NEW INFORMATION OR GAIN A NEW UNDERSTANDING. MS. SOMERVILL GREW UP IN NEW YORK STATE, BUT HAS ALSO LIVED IN TORONTO, CANADA; CANBERRA, AUSTRALIA; CALIFORNIA; AND SOUTH CAROLINA. SHE CURRENTLY LIVES WITH HER HUSBAND IN SIMPSONVILLE, SOUTH CAROLINA.